THE COLOR
OF CULTURE

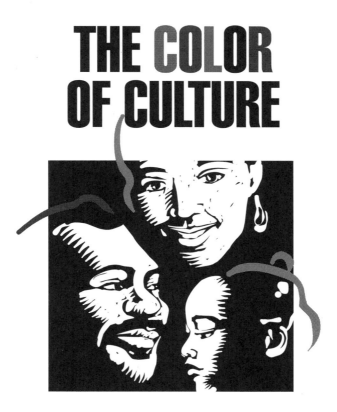

Mona Lake Jones

The Color of Culture

Second Edition
First Printing 1999

Library of Congress Catalogue number 92-076122
ISBN: 0-9635605-9-X

Manufactured in the United States of America

All of the poems and phrases featured in
The *Color of Culture* are the original
work of Mona Lake Jones

Cover Design and Illustration by Gable Design Group

Printed on recycled paper

*I dedicate this book to
Joe, Brent, Dana and especially
Sylvester and Pauline*

The Color of Culture

Culture . . .

Everybody has culture, even though some folks
think they don't. Culture is ever present.
It greets you when you and the sun first wake
up in the morning and it rests with you when
you get comfortable enough to fall asleep and
say the day is over. Culture is how you love
and who you choose to love. It's whether you
eat cornbread or pumpernickle. It's how you
respond to the dilemmas life offers and how you
celebrate living. It shows itself without you
knowing and it tells who you are without you
speaking. Culture includes all your family,
even those who are dead and gone because
they are the ones who set the cultural patterns
you follow.

Culture is often vibrant and loud or sometimes
quiet and subtle, but you know it when you see
it because it has color!

. . . Mona Lake Jones

BLACK CULTURE

One day I heard somebody say that Blacks were culturally deprived
And I wondered how they had arrived at that conclusion

I was confused by what they said
And it kept rumbling through my head

But it only took a while
Before I began to smile

You see I figured they simply didn't know
Black folks got sure 'nuff culture from our head down to our toe

It's the music that we sing and the style in which we talk
It's the preachin' and the prayin' and even the way we walk

It's the get-down way we move when the band begins to play
And the looks we give each other without using words to say

M-m-m and M-m are some ways we communicate
That folks outside our culture may not appreciate

It's how we put the man on and he doesn't even know
It's the way we keep on tryin' when someone tells us "no"

When they say we don't appreciate the finer things in life
I know, through all my education, toils and strife

I recognize good music when I hear it on the air
And to say gospel, jazz and blues aren't culture isn't fair

With James Brown, my brother, you know I've got soul
And, frankly, I often find string quartet performances rather cold

I surely recognize the finest there is in food
I don't even have to be in any special mood

To appreciate greens, black-eyed peas, cornbread and red Kool-aid
I'd turn down caviar no matter how much they paid

It's our Afros, curls and the way we do our hair
The clothes and the fashionable styles we wear

It's the sisters and the brothers struggling for the cause
Fighting economics, politics and unjust laws

But most of all,
it's the way we hang together and the kinship that we feel
That makes our culture so natural and so real

When I think about our Blackness and what our culture is all about
It's hard to keep on talking, 'cause I think I'm going to shout

"Black folks don't have any culture," I heard somebody say
And I just put my hand on my hip, rolled my eyes
and looked the other way.

THE MELTDOWN

Some folks still have the pot on the stove and have even turned up the heat.

VANISHED

An old man asked, "Before you go,
     can I tell you some history I think you should know?"

The boy answered, "I'm in a hurry, on my way out to play
     Perhaps later I could hear what you say."

A grandmother said, "Come sit my dear,
     I have something I think you should hear."

The girl over her shoulder stopped to chime
     "Maybe tomorrow I'll have the time."

And so it went and the years passed on
     Before he knew it the old man was gone

The grandmother soon went away, too
     And took with her all the wisdom she knew

When the boy and girl were older and grown
     They wished for the stories the old folks had known.

LIFE IS SWEET!

It's a dish of warm berry pie
with fresh cream melting on the top
Tasting so good you have to tell
yourself to stop.
Life is so sweet ...
Sometimes you need to pause for a
cool drink of water
Because the sweetness is almost more
than you can stand.

Life is sweet!
It makes your body shake with joy
and stirs your soul
When happiness reaches in and takes hold.
Life is so sweet ...
Sometimes you just have to lie
still and contemplate
Because the sweetness is almost
more than you can stand.

Life is sweet!
It is a bed of roses
with a soft breeze blowing through
And the fragrances of life seem to be
surrounding you.
Life is so sweet ...
Sometimes you have to close
the door, or open it, to let the aromas out
Because the sweetness is almost
more than you can stand.

Life is sweet!
It's a choir singing praises to the Lord
raising their voices in rhythmic accord.
Life is so sweet ...
Sometimes you just have to clap
your hands, stomp your feet
or say, "Amen"
Because the sweetness is almost
more than you can stand.

Yes, life is sweet!

SUNRISE

I watched the sun as it lay on the horizon
peeking up
trying to decide what to put on.

It seemed not to move, then slowly stood
and the decision was obvious.

She had selected her most brilliant attire!
Against her glowing, copper skin
she wore an orange silk dress
with a gold-sequined jacket.
She stretched her long yellow gloves
toward the skies
and circled her sparkling smile with
a bright red, wide-brimmed hat.

Then she shouted, "Good Mornin'!"
Sunrise!
Sunrise!

Culture wouldn't happen if somebody didn't love
  somebody and make somebody so somebody else could carry on.

BEING THE MOTHER OF A BLACK CHILD

*Being the mother of a Black child
it ain't no easy thing
you've got to call on Jesus and listen
to the angels sing*

They said you were what? That word
is out of style
Next time they call you names
just raise your head and smile
Tell them that you're proud
of the color of your skin
What counts is not the outside wrapping
but the character within

*Being the mother of a Black child
it ain't no easy thing
You've got to call on Jesus and listen
to the angels sing*

Sometimes I lie in bed way
late at night
And I ask God -- am I doing
this thing right?
Have I given them direction?
Do they know which way to go?
Have I overdone it just a bit?
But do they really know
They can't do just half a job
and barely pass the test?
They have to go beyond the call
and be the very best
Lord knows I've been to school
a thousand times or more
Every time the teachers look up
I'm standing in the door

But someone's got to help folks understand
how smart Black children are
And expect them not to fail, but
to reach up for a star

Being the mother of a Black child
it ain't no easy thing
You've got to call on Jesus and listen
to the angels sing

I used to put the children down
between my legs to brush a kinky head
I'd be preaching and teaching
hoping they were listening to what I said
'Cause I told them there would be
those who would tug, pull and grin
And flaunt their evil ways tempting them to sin
Because of being Black some would
give them little chance to win this game of life
And often, times would be so hard
and hours filled with strife
They would have to learn to
get down on their knees and pray
And understand, although we may not
be listening, God hears everything they say.

Being the mother of a Black child
it ain't no easy thing
You've got to call on Jesus and listen
to the angels sing

For those of you who have raised them up
or are in the process now
You surely deserve to stand and take
yourself a bow
But don't think the task is over, and
that your job is through
'Cause now you've got to reach down
and help a mother who may be struggling
just like you
You must let her know that little
Black girl or boy
Will do so many things to fill
the heart with joy
Help her realize the good they
bring will far surpass the tears
And that she will soon be looking back
thanking God for all the happy years.

Yes, being the mother of a Black child
it ain't no easy thing
You've got to call on Jesus and listen
to the angels sing

FREEDOM!

"Freedom, freedom, freedom!"
They just kept shouting, *"Freedom!"*

But there were no chains around their ankles
Their bodies were not bent nor whipped from abuse
They appeared to be exercised and strong
Yet they just kept shouting, *"Freedom!"*

They were not crying because of empty stomachs
They lived in comfortable dwellings on ordinary streets
And they looked to be fine
Yet they just kept shouting, *"Freedom!"*

It must have been their minds I was not seeing
If their minds were in bondage, struggling not to be intimidated,
ignored, confused, constricted and conquered

Then that could have prompted their cry
And that could have caused them to shout
"Freedom, freedom, freedom!"

He sat quietly, silenced by the weight of living.

OUR FUTURE

She is a sweet thing with eyes
    that twinkle when she looks
      and she is our future

He is a beautiful child with lips
    That glisten as he babbles and coos
      and he is our future

How will they grow and who will
    teach them to look with their eyes
      to find the right direction?
        And how will they know what to say?

Their ways are childlike now but soon
    he will enter manhood and she will become
      a woman. Then they will be expected to
        speak about the injustice they see and
        praise the goodness they find.

A ROOM FULL OF SISTERS

A room full of sisters, like jewels in a crown
Vanilla, cinnamon and dark chocolate brown . . .

Now picture yourself in the midst of this glory
As I describe the sisters who are part of this story.

They were wearing purples, royal blues and all shades of reds
Some had elegant hats on their heads.

With sparkling eyes and shiny lips
They moved through the room swaying their hips.

Speaking with smiles on their African faces
Their joy and laughter filled all the spaces.

They were fashionable and stylish in what they were wearing
Kind sisters who were loving and caring.

You see, it's not about how these sisters appeared
Their beauty was in the values they revered.

They were smart, articulate and well-read
With all kinds of Black history stored in their heads

Jugglers of professions, managers of lives
Mothers of children, lovers and wives

Good-hearted reaching out to others
Giving back to the community and supporting our brothers.

All of these sisters struggled the path
Suffered from prejudice, endured the wrath.

But they brushed off their dresses and pushed on the door
And they came back stronger than they were before.

Now, imagine if you will
The essence and thrill

As you stand feeling proud
In the heart of this crowd

A sisterhood of modern Sojourners today
Still out in front blazing the way.

A room full of sisters like jewels in a crown
Vanilla, cinnamon and dark chocolate brown.

JUST BETWEEN US

This is just between us -- nobody else needs to know
You must promise this is as far as it will go!

When I saw Clara whispering to Lucille in
church last week
I knew sure enough there would be a leak.

I think Fannie was the original source,
But she confided in her best friend Sally, of course.

When Jane came in and asked Sally, "What's new?"
Sally told Jane and Jane told Sue.

Sue didn't keep it for more than a day,
'Cause she called Jean and Jean called May.

Now, when May gave the news to Esther,
Esther told Bea.
That's how the story got to me.

The way the news got out is really a shame
If you tell somebody else --
please don't use my name!

It doesn't matter which door you came in. What counts
is what you do once you're inside.

CHICKEN AND DUMPLINS'

Something was cooking in the big iron pot
I slipped into the kitchen and said, "Mama, what you got?"

"It's especially for you, baby. It's just what you need."
I opened the pot and said, "Ooo, wee, yes indeed!"

It was my favorite chicken and dumplins', the kind you
barely have to chew,
I was so tickled, I hardly knew what to do.

Mama fixed me a bowl. I planned on two or three,
'Cause she'd cooked all these chicken and dumplins'
especially for me.

I pulled up a chair and got me a seat.
I sat down to the table and was fixing to eat.

The cornbread was ready and everything was just right
When before my eyes came a terrible sight.

It was hard times Uncle Charlie and Aunt Birdie, too,
They had all five of their children, including
little sister Sue.

Uncle Charlie hadn't worked for almost a year
And little Suzie stood trying to well up a tear.

She leaned over the table and said, "It sure smells good.
I'd have some too, if I could."

Before I could speak her spoon had dipped in my bowl.
I'm telling you the truth, I was one disappointed soul.

Mama nodded her head "yes" and I just bowed mine
'Cause I knew company came first and I'd be the last in line.

Well, when they finished eating and thanked Mama real nice,
Little sister Sue even thanked her twice.

I walked over to the stove and opened up the pot
And the smell of them dumplins' is all that I got!

Culture invites you to participate in living.

DEFINITELY DANCIN'

Somebody hollered

"Git Down!"

I was def-i-nite-ly dancin'

My body was twistin' and turnin'
My hips were groovin' and movin'

I was def-i-nite-ly dancin'

My shoes were tappin' and pattin'
My hands were snappin' and clappin'

"Git Down!"

I was def-i-nite-ly dancin'

My arms were swingin' and swayin'
My legs were flippin' and kickin'

I was def-i-nite-ly dancin'

Then after a while I started perspirin' and sweatin'
My breath started puffin' and pantin'
My feet felt like they were breakin' and achin'

And then I definitely had to

"Sit Down!"

THE INTERVIEW

This morning I got up ready to get down!

My attitude was setting just right
My body felt fine
My smile was in place
And my eye was on the prize!

My thoughts were well thought
My words rehearsed
My stockings on straight
And my outfit was color-coordinated!

My resume was in order
My credentials lined up
My future plans ready to be articulated
My ability to get along with others
was evidenced by my sparkling personality
And I was on time!

I arrived and spoke with such poise
"I am here to interview for the job of assistant
to the assistant vice-president
in charge of assisting the president."

When I stepped though the door,
                          I knew the job was mine!

CHOICES

M-mm-mmm Should I demonstrate,
tolerate, educate, negotiate or just
kick ass ...?

JUST TOO SMART

They shouted: Slaves, you will always be!
But Harriet came along and said, "Shhh... through the underground
railroad, right this way."

I knowed we could do it!

They tried to keep us from voting, but we marched and organized.
"This afternoon the Congressional Black Caucus will meet in Senate
Room 155."

I knowed we could do it!

They said: Move on to the back of the bus!
"Watch your step please - fifty cents - next stop, 15th and East Cherry."

I knowed we could do it!

Not long ago, they would provide no food service, not even a seat.
"May I take your order please -- I'm sorry, we don't serve stroganoff -
would you care for some collards?"

I knowed we could do it!

They said we could work together, but surely not to live next door.
"My address? 100 Circle Park View Drive."

I knowed we could do it!

They said we weren't smart enough to learn our ABC's.
But the door cracked open - we went to Harvard, and got our Ph.D.'s.

I knowed -- I knew we could do it!

You see, our cognitive capabilities of assimilation and accommodation
are just too copious and our epistemological skills are overwhelming.

In other words -- we're just too smart!

31

IT'S LOOKING FROM THE INSIDE OUT

It's not being red, white, yellow, black or brown that makes a
woman or a man meet the challenges at hand.

It's looking from the inside out --
That's what life is all about.

It's thinking clearly with a goal in mind,
respecting others and being kind.

It's learning all that you can
and trying hard to make a plan

Making choices you think are right
then striving for the tallest height.

It's not just thinking only of you,
but caring about those around you too.

It's looking from the inside out --
That's what life is all about.

The Black boy, even off the field must wear his helmet.

OUR AFRICAN-AMERICAN CHILDREN
ARE COMING

Hurry, our African-American children are coming
Arriving by the thousands each and every day
Counting on you and me to show them the way

Hurry, now hurry!

Get to the church and tell the preacher
    they will be needing to hear God's word
And that they must be given scriptures
    for they have not yet heard

Find families who will love them and
    provide the confidence to grow
Then they can take the risk
    to learn all they need to know

Stock the shelves with books that
    tell them who they are
So they can dream that
    their success cannot be far

Hurry, now hurry!

Fix the schools so they
    expect our children to succeed
Recognition of their bright, creative minds
    is what they need

Provide their care in environments
    that help them thrive
Ones that show them they can do
    more than just survive

Pull the curtain on the peddlers of drugs
    and tell them to go away
Let them know we will give the children direction
    and guide their way

Hurry, now hurry!

Make sure the tables are set with food that
    is good for their soul
To make their bodies strong
    and ready to unfold

Change the minds of those who they will encounter
    so they look at our children with care
Respecting them by playing the games
    with rules that are fair

Gather just enough worldly goods
    to satisfy their needs
So they can keep their values focused on one another,
    sharing and doing kind deeds

Hurry, now hurry, don't you understand?
They are reaching out asking for your hand

Hurry, our African-American children are coming
    Arriving by the thousands each and every day
Counting on you and me
    to show them the way

Hurry, now hurry!

Sometimes it's hard to pretend you're not aware
that people wish you weren't there.

IF LOOKS COULD GET YOU, I'D BE GOT!

If looks could get you, I'd be got -- 'cause every time I got ready to do my thing, my Mama or my Daddy, my Grandmother or my Auntie Butler (who is no real relation to our family) would catch me, look me straight in the eye, and I would nearly die and I'd have to stop what I was doing.

I can't count the times I was nearly killed right on the church bench while the preacher was preaching. Once, all I was fixing to do was pinch Bobby so he could see Mrs. Johnson had on one of those funny-looking hats setting all to the front of her head. My Mama's eyes caught me and pierced me so hard I felt my heart stop, and I had to catch my breath!

My Grandmother, who we called Grandhoney 'cause she was so sweet, would look as if she was tickled about me being so shamed. I would try my best not to look at her, but sometimes I'd check just to see if she were sleeping and she would be looking hard, not saying a word, and I would have to adjust my agenda!

Daddy really only had to look half a look. He didn't look often and he didn't look hard. He didn't even wrinkle his forehead or squint his eyes. He just looked! I used to wish he would say something out loud so the hurt inside me would stop and I could go on with something else; but I would just stand and wait until he said, "Go on, girl."

My Auntie Butler (who is not my real aunt), I don't know how she thought she had the rights to looking. She looked more than anybody! She looked from her front porch while I was outside playing. She looked at church. She looked on my way home from school. She even looked when she saw you at the store. Auntie Butler was always causing me to change my plans.

Now, I thought when I grew up I could do my thing without anybody looking. But yesterday I was having a brief conversation on the phone with my best friend Johnetta and I happened to glance up and my HUSBAND had the nerve to be looking!!!

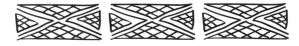

Our family is a package deal!

EASTER SUNDAY

They were the prettiest people I'd ever seen!

Their eyes were bright and their smiles wide
You could tell they were feeling special inside

Beautiful children coming to worship and pray
Were dressed in their finest for church that day

The girls had braids and curls adorned with bows
Some wore patent shoes with ribbons on the toes

Their colorful dresses were in every hue
You could tell they must have all been brand new

For they puffed them and smoothed them
            and pushed up each sleeve
And the adjustments they made, you wouldn't believe!

The boys had on suits that were bought out of fear
They could not even wear them for a full year

Their pants hung a little too long and the
            coats were not quite their size
But as fast as they were growing, I'm
            sure the choices proved to be wise

Now it was Easter Sunday and an hour had passed
It was uncertain how long the children would last

Some fell asleep and they didn't even know
That the sermon had been going an hour or so

But the boys who were awake began popping their
            suspenders and stretching their ties
They made funny faces and crossed their eyes

A few of the boys proved they were men
When they unlaced their shoes and then tied them again

When one little girl twisted her hair
Her sister told her she looked funny and she said "I don't care!"

It was the second hour they were truly put to the test
And each was challenged to behave at their best

Some counted their fingers and squirmed in their seat
Sucked their thumbs and danced their feet

They loosened their collars and unbuttoned their shirts
They took out their bows and fanned their skirts

But when the Easter service finally came to an end
And the children stood to say their final "Amen"

They looked a bit different, slightly askew
But the beauty in their faces still shown through

They were the prettiest people I'd ever seen!

Likin' is nice, but lovin' is a whole lot better.

THE NECESSITIES OF LIFE

Love provides plenty of food for thought
and when you drink it in, it quenches your thirst.
Love affords you the opportunity
to exercise if you reach out, pull in, lift up
and then relax and take in a deep breath.
When you're wrapped up in *Love*, it gives shelter
and when you hold on to it,
Love can be a retreat from the realities of living.
Love can soothe the hurt and provide the
strength you need for the struggle.

DELICATE PASSION

It was only just a touch
It wasn't really very much

But when you whispered what you said
The words went dancing through my head.

I started to grin
I could hardly keep it in.

All that happy bubbling way down deep
Suddenly began to creep.

I felt my heart beat at a quicker pace.
And a smile came on my face

I was glad no one could see how uncontrolled I was.
All of this was happening because
I remembered how it felt when you touched me!

It was only just a touch
It wasn't really very much

But when you pressed against me slightly
And for a moment squeezed my hand so tightly

I looked into your eyes and I was so surprised to find
You had a feeling just like mine.

Now I'm thinking of tonight
When I've planned everything just right.

For the first time we can be alone to explore
And discover if there is something more

Than the simple little touch
We first thought wasn't really very much!

I looked everywhere. Then
I found my true love living right around the corner on
37th & Jefferson.

SNIGGLIN' AND GIGGLIN'

Snigglin' and gigglin' down
under the covers way late
at night

Me and my man were just
Snigglin' and gigglin'

Sniggle, giggle

   Sniggle giggle

      Sniggle

       Sniggle

Sni-i-ggle

        Oh-oh -- this ain't no laughin' matter!

THE APOLOGY

Baby, I didn't do it on purpose"
    and then he kissed me on my forehead

"Baby, I didn't mean to do it"
    and then he kissed me on my lips

"Baby, I didn't intend to hurt your feelings"
    and then he kissed me all up and
        down my neck

"Baby, I know I shouldn't have done it"
    and then he kissed me across
        my shoulders

"Baby, I'm sorry!"
    and then he kissed me and kissed me
        and kissed me ...

And I was almost glad he had done what he did!

BROKEN HEART

She danced into his life, tapped
on his heart, twirled him
around her finger, sidestepped
and then shuffled away.

A PROMISE OF LOVE

It may have been a look or glance
that later turned into romance.

Or perhaps it was a spoken word or two
that happened long before they really knew

That their relationship would grow
into the friendship they now know.

It might have been just the way they cared
or a special moment that was shared.

Could it have been the times each made
the other laugh or cry
that proved to be the reason why

That even through their times of strife
They promised to commit their love for life?

They may never clearly understand
how their love first began.

But they are certain of what they feel now
and will stand to make their wedding vow

May happiness follow in all they do
and God, bless the union of these two.

SMILE

Keeping a smile ready is something that should be done
Especially if you're looking to meet the right one

> Try your smile out on folks who pass
> even when you think they may not count
>
> Practice your smile when no one is looking
> to make sure you can use it when it's time
>
> Demonstrate your smile for those
> who don't seem to know how it works
>
> Keep your smile out in the open
> so you can quickly get to it when the moment's right
>
> Be generous with your smile
> because you have so many needing to be used
>
> Combine your smile with a kind word
> to increase your opportunity for a response

Knowing you have met the right one will be determined
by what they do
It just depends on whether they keep your smile
or choose to give it back to you!

Question: Who is responsible for all that which needs fixing?

Answer: "They are!"

Question: "Well, who is going to fix it?"

Answer: "You and me!"

THE CHALLENGE OF PERPLEXITY

Sometimes I like to sit perplexed
and wonder what may be coming next.

It seems to give importance to my being,
when I am not clearly seeing.

I often have the need to ponder
and to let my mind roam and wander,

Looking for concrete words to say
why things are this way.

I find it difficult to draw conclusions,
because reality mixes with my illusions.

And when my thinking becomes blurred,
that is when my greatest solutions have occurred.

It is at that moment,
when I have examined all that is at stake,
that I have figured out which path to take.

I am glad when my prediction has come true
and it turns out that I knew!

But when life decides to take a different turn,
then I view it as a lesson learned.

And once again,
sometimes I like to sit perplexed,
and wonder what may be coming next . . .

BROTHERS

It was Saturday morning around about ten
When I was passing the barber shop and I happened to look in.

My heart skipped a beat when I saw through the door
And I moved in closer so I could hear a little more.

The shop had culture just bursting at the seam
And when I tell you what I saw, you'll know what I mean.

There were brothers of all ages sitting waiting in line
Each one of them I would describe as fine!

Now I don't mean fine because they were short, tall or thin
I mean these were genuinely handsome Black men.

Their love and strength showed in their eyes
You knew, for some, years of living had made them wise.

They were daddies, uncles, grandpas, young men and one small son
Laughing, talking and having great fun!

The most beautiful example of the love that they shared
Was when they showed the one small son how they cared.

For the very first time this little fella was sitting in the chair
And the barber was fixing to cut his hair.

Even with his father standing close by
When the clippers were turned on he started to cry.

He had fear in his eyes and tears rolled down his face
And I'm happy I was there to see what took place.

First, old Brother Smith's hand, wrinkled from the years
Reached down and wiped away the small boy's tears.

With his hand on his shoulder brother Brown said, "Look here, son.
This has happened to everyone."

There was love in the hearts of the brothers that day
They knew what to do and just what to say.

Some told stories about when they were little men
And how they still get frightened every now and then.

Those brothers created tales that I've never heard
And the small boy sat listening to every word.

They talked about things I knew he couldn't understand
'Cause they were tales that should have been told a grown man.

They spoke about the politics of today and last year
And the upcoming elections that were drawing near.

They bragged about their cars, the new ones and old
And about the Rolls Royce that Smitty claimed he had on hold!

They demonstrated slam dunks, home runs and how
    touchdowns were scored
And the small boy sat and never looked bored.

When they talked about the pretty women with the big fat thighs
I knew half of those stories had to be lies.

'Cause old brother Brady was almost eighty-five
And if his stuff wasn't dead, you knew it was barely alive!

I couldn't help but smile as each one of them spoke
And I found myself laughing aloud when they told
    their outrageous jokes.

Now the barber had been cutting all this while
And when he announced he was finished,
    the small boy started to smile.

These brothers had done all that they could
And the little boy seemed to have understood.

The boy looked at his elders with such awe
Admiration and proudness is what I saw.

Before he got down the brothers each shook his hand
And they told him he was a fine Black man!

Now when his Daddy got up to take his turn
He didn't flinch or blink, he just sat looking stern.

The scissors started clicking and the boy
    put his hand on his Dad's knee
Looked up and said, "Daddy, you can do it just like me."

When his Dad was finished, he picked up the boy
They stood looking in the mirror
    and you could sense their joy.

Dad smiled when his son whispered in his ear
As if he didn't want the others to hear.

But when the boy raised his fingers, you knew then
He'd said, "Now, Daddy, there are two fine Black men!"

I could go on with this story 'cause there is so much to say
But I left with happiness in my heart that day.

Convinced that there are simply no others
Who can take the place of our fine Black Brothers!

TRANSITION

He was a
round
brown
bouncing
baby
boy
What a joy!

Now he's a
long
lanky
leathery
luscious
man
ain't it grand!

UNCLE THOMAS

How did his mind get so twisted
and who does he think he is?

When did he forget where he came from
and who helped him attain his position in life?

What made him begin to feel he was someone better
and who convinced him he was different from his brothers?

How could he forget the generations that came before his time
and how did he lose sight of the sacrifices each made on his behalf?

Why doesn't he use his talents to lift the community he has now left behind
and why is he always grinning, pretending to be having such fun?

How can he not feel compassion or the need to be reaching back and how in
the world is he able to imagine being anything other than **Black**!

HEAVENLY RECALL

When Mother Nature finished painting the
    beautiful new colors for fall
She announced she had also been sent to
    conduct a heavenly recall

She stood to get attention and
    then majestically raised her brush
The people on earth stopped what they were
    doing and suddenly there was a hush

It seemed there had been some mistakes made
    between the years 1910 and 1997
The coloring instructions were misguided
    as they traveled down from heaven

Some people had been colored Black
    who should have been painted White
And Mother Nature was now here to see
    that things were done right

"If you think your color is wrong and
    White is what you should be
Just step to the front of the crowd,
    I'll change your color for free."

Mother Nature brought gallons and gallons
    of paint that was white
And was surrounded by angels in case, during
    the rush, folks started to fight

One child tried to move forward
    But her mother jerked her back
And said, "Girl, you're confused, we just started
    teaching you why you're glad to be Black"

A man raised his hand then quickly put it down
        When those standing by looked startled
And some even began to frown

He mumbled, "I didn't quite hear the directions
        I misunderstood what was said."
Then he put his hand in his pocket and
        shamefully hung his head.

There were a few shoulders that shrugged and some
        bodies that swayed
But those were the only movements they made

Those up for recall chose to stand solid
        as if they were stuck
And after a while, the angels began
        loading the paint back in the truck

The people shouted, "Yes, take that paint back
        We like who we are and we are
proud to be Black."

"We refuse the offer to all be painted White
        Changing our color will not make
things right"

Mother Nature put the truck into gear,
        smiled and they all drove away
But said they would return on the
        first winter day

"Don't worry," the angels shouted, "For you
        will be pleased
We can use the white paint to put snow
        on the mountains and trees."

God just keeps on giving me another chance.

CHANGE

Put a period in your life
       and make a fresh start
Exercise your mind
       and open up your heart.

Think of all the things
       that you may want to do
Throw out those clothes that make you dreary
       and dress up in something new.

Focus on the future
       and stop turning to look back
Pack your bags and board a train
       traveling on a different track.

Don't be afraid to take the chance,
       to make another turn
Just imagine all that lies ahead
       and the opportunities to learn.

Step out in front and
       pick up the pace
Smooth the wrinkles in your brow and
       put a smile on your face

Plan a way to use your talents
       to create a better earth
Then let the outcomes of your efforts
       show how much you're worth.

Once you have decided
       to move with a different stride
Just knowing how far you've come
       will make you walk with pride.

Remember, you can't wait for others
       to applaud what you do
So just congratulate yourself and
       then start something new!

The Color of Culture

IMPACT COMMUNICATIONS
Seattle, Washington